NIGERIA:

*A Decade of Sycophancy, Waste, and
Looting of Public Funds (1999 - 2009)*

NIGERIA:

A Decade of Sycophancy, Waste, and
Looting of Public Funds (1999 - 2009)

AGBAI INA OBASI

(BA, JD IN LAW)

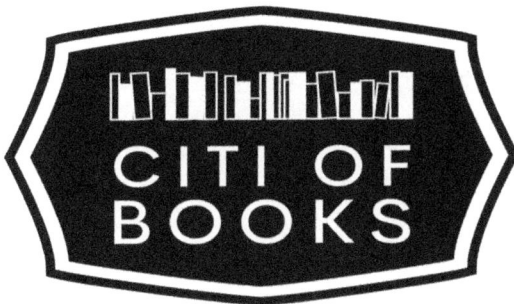

CITI OF
BOOKS

CITIOFBOOKS, INC.
3736 Eubank NE Suite A1
Albuquerque, NM 87111-3579
www.citiofbooks.com
Hotline: 1 (877) 389-2759
Fax: 1 (505) 930-7244

Ordering Information:
Quantity Sales. Special discounts are available on quantity purchases by corporations, associations, and others. For details, contact the publisher at the address above.

Printed in the United States of America.

ISBN-13   Paperback   978-1-959682-02-8
                 eBook   978-1-959682-03-5

Library of Congress Control Number: 2022919289

Author's Contact Details
Email Address: ina_obasi@yahoo.com
Contact Number: 9195617648

CONTENTS

DEDICATION

—⟨•/•/•⟩—

This book is especially dedicated to:

Chy, Ina, Stephy/Nnenna, Uba, and my mother who have always been there to encourage and support me through thick and thin.

The Obasi Brothers family especially our patriarchs and Matriarchs—Chief Ina E. Obasi (Ekwueme Abiriba), Chief Uba E. Obasi, (Ochi Oha Abiriba), Chief Mrs. Tai Ina Obasi and Elder Mrs. Kalaria Uba Obasi in recog-nition of their services to the Abiriba community and humanity at large.

All Nigerians wherever they may be, who have suffered and are still suffering untold hardship at the hands of their corrupt leaders;

The growing number of readers of my books worldwide, who have encouraged me to write more.

God bless you all.

How Much Money Does One Really Need to Live a Comfortable Life?

With 100 million, 50 million, 25million, or 10 million naira in a fixed deposit at an interest rate of 6 percent PA, one can be spending 500,000, 250,000, 125,000, and 50,000 Naira, respectively, every month without ever touching the fixed principal amount.

If only our leaders knew this and would realize that the world is only a transit point and not our final destination, perhaps this recklessness in looting public funds and primitive accumulation of wealth would be minimized.

INTRODUCTION

―――∞∞∞――――

THIS BOOK TRIES TO HIGHLIGHT SOME OF the major events of the decade ending in 2009, which portrayed the depth to which Nigeria had gone in self-destruction. As you read on, you will be touched and shocked by the neglect, abuse, and impunity heaped on this nation and the show of greed, which had gone beyond greed to madness, both in the public and the private sectors.

Some African leaders had gone to God to complain about the seeming unfairness in the distribution of natural and human resources in Africa, especially in the West African subregion in favor of Nigeria, and God responded, "Wait until you see the people that I will put in there." This joke aptly summarized the tragedy that has fallen on this naturally endowed sleeping giant of Africa called Nigeria. It is difficult to describe in words what happened to this once flourishing country that carried high the aspirations and hopes of every African about five decades ago.

The reason for this downward trend is obvious and is illustrated with numerous examples throughout the book. A major cause of this is what I describe as our collective sycophancy.

Quoting from my book titled *Financial Independence:* ***"Sycophancy is a disease that has turned our citizenry into a docile lot, willingly accepting the atrocities committed by our leaders."***

While some Nigerians are content with just a meal of rice and chicken for their support in this unwholesome war against our nation, for others, sycophancy has become a profession whose practitioners are engaged in fanning the greed of our leaders for their selfish interest to the detriment of our collective well-being. There seems to be no end in sight as each day brings out the worst in our polit-ical class. It is my hope that as we read this book, we Nigerians will begin to collectively review our conduct and gradually resist this evil that has befallen our nation.

We can begin by frowning on such behaviors of our leaders that are detrimental to our collective aspirations. This will be followed by our collective resistance and expression of disgust toward these unacceptable behaviors. We will then insist on accountability and transparency from our leaders and that adequate punishment be meted out to all those found culpable.

After reading this book, I hope that you will be encouraged to join the fight against this monstrous sycophancy, waste, and looting of public funds that have retarded our development and help put the nation back on the path of sustainable development.

THE ELECTION OF 1999.

—∞∞∞—

The government of General Olusegun Obasanjo started on a good note with the reshuffling of the Army that, at that point, had become so powerful, politicized, and corrupt that it would take a man with a fearless heart to tamper with and reorganize it.

Another of the General's success stories at this early stage of his administration was in the area of financial prudence. The appointment of the former World Bank executive who spearheaded the debt repayment of the country was a welcome relief.

AFTER THE JUNE 12 SAGA AND THE annulment of the freest election ever in the country in 1993, there was a lot of pressure on the ruling military junta to douse the tension in the western part of Nigeria. Thus, when the Peoples Democratic Party of Nigeria (PDP) selected the General as its candidate in the 1999 general election, a lot of people felt relieved. Most people were sympathetic, not because of the General's past track record as a former head of state of Nigeria, but because they felt that he would have been reformed by his near-death experience during his long jail term. The people erroneously believed that his disposition to human rights and life in general would have been changed by the inhuman torture and suffering meted out to him during his unwarranted incarceration. So they came out and supported his candidacy even without any financial inducement, as the general was almost bankrupt at that time by his own testimony. This is very unlike what happens in Nigerian politics where financial and material inducements play a dominant role in getting peoples' support in an election. So the election came, and despite its flaws, it could be said that General Olusegun Obasanjo won the popular vote against his opponents. The swearing-in ceremony was very colorful, and Nigerians witnessed the coming of another civilian government after about sixteen years of military rule.

The General's government started on a good note with the reshuffling of the army that had become so powerful, politicized, and corrupt that it would take a man with a fearless heart to tamper with and reorganize it. Within the first few months of the administration, the general made sweeping changes and sent most of the corrupt, "political" soldiers to retirement.

In his attempt to fight corruption, the General established many agencies charged with the onerous task of fighting all shades of corruption that was endemic in the society. Among the outstanding agencies were the Economic and Financial Crimes Commission (EFCC) and the National Agency for Food and Drug Administration and Control (NAFDAC). The success stories of these two agencies, especially NAFDAC, were unparalleled in the history of fighting corruption in the country. At this time, fake drug dealerships had become a very lucrative business throughout the country despite its devastating effects on the lives of many Nigerians. With passion, commitment and determination, the then director general of NAFDAC pursued her job and achieved unparalleled success despite threats to her life and that of her family; the same could be said about the EFFC boss, especially at the initial stage. For the first time in Nigeria, fighting corruption was at the front burner of our national discourse. People began to feel and express the slogan that "the fear of EFCC is the beginning of wisdom."

Another success story of the General at this early stage of his administration was in the area of financial prudence. The appointment of a former World Bank executive who spearheaded the debt repayment of the country was a welcome relief. Not only was the national debt repaid, the excess funds generated from the sales of crude were saved, despite the pressure from stakeholders to distribute the funds among them.

While all these were going on and the economy seemed to be responding positively with external investment flowing into the country, the politicians who seemed left out of the scheme of things began to make their sycophantic moves. The first move was to convince the General that "he was the best thing that ever happened to the country. Consequently, he must run for a second term."

THE SECOND TERM OPTION AND THE ABANDONMENT OF INFRASTRUCTURAL DEVELOPMENT

———◈◈◈———

In a trap like this, the General had to succumb to the greed of the sycophants who stood to benefit from the pursuit of the General's second term ambition.

The adage "whom the cap fits, let him wear it" became generally accepted by the populace to the detriment of the nation whose developmental funds were allegedly converted to campaign funds. For the General to achieve his ambition, he had to build a loyal base in the party and amass a financial fortune to fight the opposition in the party.

Once the General bought into this idea of a second-term, the sycophants had succeeded in their plot to derail the new administration barely two years into its four-year term.

HAVING CONVINCED THE GENERAL THAT "THE cap fits him" and he must run a second-term, the political sycophants were faced with the issue of modalities. Recall that the General was an out-sider in the PDP prior to the election of 2003. Therefore, getting him to run a second time in the general election in 2003 was not going to be an easy sell to the party. There were a lot more financially powerful people within the party, who had supported the candidacy of the General in 1999 on the understanding that he would only serve for one term. These people were going to oppose the General's second term.

In a scenario like this, the General had to succumb to the greed of the sycophants who stood to benefit from the pursuit of his (the General's) second-term ambition. The adage "whom the cap fits let him wear it" became generally accepted to the detriment of the welfare of the populace.

For the General to achieve his ambition, he had to build a loyal base in the party and amass a financial fortune to fight the opposition in the party. Once he bought this idea of a second term, the political sycophants had succeeded in their plot to derail the new administration barely two years into its four-year term. To raise the needed funds, huge contracts would have to be awarded to these loyal political sycophants; so appointments were made into positions that would generate the needed funds. It was alleged that several billions of Naira budgeted for contracts on road repairs and maintenance were diverted for this second-term agenda.

Critics have alleged that this was the beginning of the abandonment of the Lagos–Benin Highway reconstruction which to date is still a death trap for road users despite the fact that it is the number one highway in the country. This road has an increasing toll of fatal accidents, intensifying public outcry for reconstruction. A journey that would ordinarily take less than six hours from Lagos to the eastern part of the country sometimes takes a whole day. It has become a nightmare for road users. So were other major highways in the nation abandoned like the Enugu–Aba-Port Harcourt.

The story is the same for other infrastructures in the country, notably: the electric power supply, the educational system, provision of healthcare, and other sectors of the economy. No sector was spared. I will briefly highlight a few of these sectors that have adversely affected the lives of the majority of Nigerians. The decay in our educational and health sectors is better imagined than seen. Our hospitals have now turned to death traps. The school system, in the face of meager government funding, had turned our Ivory Towers into citadels of corruption. Corruption is visible everywhere in the school system from the admission system to the teaching, grading, and passing of exams. Our universities have been turned into an environment worse than Sodom and Gomorrah. Yet every year, the system graduates thousands of half-baked, ill-equipped candidates into the workforce that will join the queue of existing growing numbers of unemployed, who are vying for survival and the acquisition of ill-gotten riches.

Electricity supply had gone from bad to worse despite huge sums of money allegedly invested in the power sector. The total number of megawatts available to the nation has remained less than three thousand megawatts in the decade despite the vast increase in population and the rapidly expanding housing sector. The rot in this sector (electric power supply) would be exposed by the House of Representatives power probe in a later chapter. The whole country is consequently like a gigantic factory run on power generators day and night. No wonder the attendant atmospheric and environmental pollution and the health hazards they constitute to Nigerians are unparalleled.

These are some of the consequences of the political sycophants' successes in cornering our leaders for their selfish goals. Here, they got what they wanted, which is maintaining a corrupt society by giving the General what he wanted: a second term in power.

THE NATIONAL ASSEMBLY.

———◦/◦/◦———

In a space of ten years, the Assembly had witnessed numerous changes in their leadership, most of which was allegedly instigated by the executive arm of the government.

These frequent changes in the leadership of the National Assembly had denied the Assembly the ability to develop the leadership skills required to effectively perform their constitutional functions, much to the delight of the instigators.

The most notorious of these scandals was the one involving Etteh, the last speaker of the House. Unlike the other scandals, this speaker dragged the whole nation into this unfortunate and shameless incident popularly referred to as the "Ettehgate Scandal."

Our presidential system of government makes provision for a "division of governmental powers into the three branches—Legislative, Executive, and Judiciary—each with specified powers and duties of which neither of the other branches can encroach.

—*Black Law Dictionary* by Bryan Garner

7

THIS DIVISION OF POWER IS ENSHRINED IN the military imposed 1999 Constitution of the Federal Republic of Nigeria in the separation of powers clause that empowers the legislature to make laws for the good governance of the nation. The legislature is composed of the Senate and the House of Representatives. While representation in the Senate is based on equality of the states, the House is based mostly on the population ratio in the federal constituencies.

However, the decade witnessed a National Assembly that was subservient, unfocused, self-centered, disorderly, and corrupt. From the beginning, there were attempts by the executive branch to exert its influence on the legislature. Initially this was firmly resisted by the members of the National Assembly, who even went a step further by instituting an impeachment proceeding against the over-bearing General in his first-term of office.

However, the impeachment process was abandoned when former heads of state, elder statesmen, traditional rulers, and some other political sycophants within and outside the government appealed to the leadership of the National Assembly to abandon their course of action. After that, the National Assembly was never the same as they timidly succumbed to the dictates of the General from then on. But never in his eight years in power had the General been put under such pressure as he had been with the impeachment attempt. For the first time, the General was scared and shocked to the bones. As expected, the duo of Anyim (The Senate President) and Na'abba (The Speaker of the House), who spearheaded the impeachment proceedings, just like Nnamani, another Senate President, would be forced to exit the Assembly but with the admiration of the people.

In a space of ten years, the Assembly had witnessed numerous changes in leadership; most of which were allegedly instigated by the executive arm of government. From Enwerem to Mark in the Senate and from Buhari to Bankole in the House, the story was the same. There were six and five leadership changes in the Senate and in the House, respectively, within the decade. These frequent changes in the leadership of the National Assembly had denied the Assembly the ability to develop leadership skills required to effectively perform their constitutional functions, to the delight of the instigators. Thus, independent-minded leaders like Okadigbo, Nnamani, Anyim, and Na'abba were all forced out of the Assembly.

Unable to demonstrate its independence from the executive arm, the National Assembly members settled down to take care of themselves. Thus, the Assembly was engulfed in numerous scandals involving inflated contract awards, excessive appropriation of emoluments to Assembly members, centering on housing and constituency allowances and misappropriations of public funds by its leadership, especially in the House of Representatives.

A more notorious case was the scandal involving Etteh, the last speaker of the House. Unlike the other scandals, this speaker dragged the whole nation into this unfortunate and shameless incident popularly referred to as "the Ettehgate Scandal." I remember watching the incident on a cable TV reality show in the United States, called the "Disorder in the National Assembly." On the TV show, I saw this huge member of the House, 6 feet, 3 inches and 290 pounds, standing on a table and delivering a series of heavy punches to the head of his opponent standing on the floor, who was in support of removing the speaker. It was funny, seeing this huge man in his traditional attire made with twelve yards of cloth materials popularly called *babariga*, dragged down from the table to receive multiples of punches in return, leaving him fleeing for safety with a bloody nose.

He learned the hard way not to fight with that kind of ceremonial attire, which hindered his fighting/self-defense skills. As the commotion was going on, Etteh was led out of the committee room by security officers of the National Assembly.

While the Assembly had spent much of its time to discuss housing, constituency, and other allowances, changing leadership, and struggling for committee chairman positions; they neglected their primary function of making laws for the good governance of the country. Consequently, bills like the freedom of the press bill was pending in the Assembly for years.

THE ELECTION OF 2003.

It was indeed a mockery of democracy where elections were won not by the people's vote but by manipulations, threats, inducement, and rigging.

During the elections, there was violence everywhere you went. Ballot boxes were snatched and destroyed in full view of security officers. Ballot papers were thumb-printed outside the voting areas and transported to the collection centers with official escorts.

How can this sham be called an elec-tion when people's votes did not count? Surprisingly, the judiciary affirmed most of the results of this massively rigged election.

THE QUASI-ELECTION THAT ENSUED IN 2003 became one of the worst ever conducted in the country up until that time. The campaigns were not based on any political ideology but a show of brute force and financial inducement. I recall an incident where the General went on a campaign rally in the eastern part of the country. Mounting the campaign stand, the General issued a threat to the mammoth crowd that came to listen to him. He commanded them in his usual imperial fashion to call to order one of their illustrious sons, who happened to be the Senate president then. The man had fallen out of favor with the General because of his principled stand on issues and the earlier mentioned botched impeachment of the General. The General declared that if they (the people) did not call the then-president of the Senate to order, he would be forced to use the police and the army if need be to restore order in his own way. It is grossly ironical that this kind of campaign speech would be made by a candidate who was supposedly asking for the people's vote.

The opposition in the ruling party (PDP) to which the General belonged had an opportunity not to return him as presidential candidate in the Party's National Convention. It was alleged that the governors had ganged up with the then-vice president (Atiku) against the General with the aim of returning a former vice president (Ekwueme) as the presidential candidate for the election. The plot thickened, and it was evident that the General would not survive the plot. However, twenty-four hours before the party convention, the then-vice president reached an understanding with the General and convinced the governors to vote for the General at the party convention. This decision, which gave the General a new lease of political power, would haunt the then vice president for a long time to come.

The relegation of the populace during the election campaign happened throughout the country; no meaningful issues were raised or discussed during the campaign. The election was not going to be decided on that but, rather, by the financial inducement of the electoral officers, threat to use brute force on the masses, and, of course, other elec-tion rigging tactice.

During the elections, there was violence everywhere you went. Ballot boxes were snatched and destroyed in full view of the security officers. Ballot papers were thumb-printed outside the voting areas and transported to the collation centers with official escorts. Both local and foreign observers of the election adjudged it substantially rigged. Yet nothing was done to redress the wrong. Thereafter, the political sycophants came up with a new slogan: "Let's give peace and our nascent democracy a chance." This slogan dominated public discourse for a while in an attempt to justify inaction against the massive rigging that characterized the 2003 general elections. People who insisted on the rule of law were treated as enemies of the state and ruthlessly dealt with.

Needless to say, the election came and went, returning all the elective officers, except the candidates in opposition to the ruling party (PDP), who were unable to muster enough resources to rig themselves back to power.

At the conclusion of this quasi-election, the PDP-controlled states increased, and their strangle-hold on the people became more dominant. However, there were a few instances where former members of the PDP broke ranks with the party to form another party and still regained their elective positions due to their ability to outrig the dominant PDP in those particular locations like in Lagos (AC) and Abia (PPC) states.

It was indeed a mockery of democracy where elections were won not by the people's vote but by manipulations, threats, inducements, and rigging. How can this sham be called an election when people's votes did not count? Surprisingly, the judiciary affirmed most of the results of this massively rigged election.

THE EMPEROR (GENERAL OLUSEGUN OBASANJO)

—ⲟⲛⲟ—

With the party and executive power solidly behind him, the Emperor began to fish out and torment oppositions within and outside the party (PDP). The EFCC that had started on a good note was turned into a ruthless war machine against the opposition (real or imagined)..

In pursuit of his third-term ambition, the Emperor beamed his searchlight on his vice president who had helped him win the party primary at the 2003 party convention.

For selfish political reasons and in an unprecedented defiance of the highest court of the land, the Emperor seized and would not release the statutory allocation of Lagos state, notwithstanding its adverse consequences on the economy of the state and the sufferings of its citizenry.

WITH THE ELECTION OF 2003 OVER, THE General started the consolidation of power to himself. Recall in 1999, he was an outsider in the party.

With his reelection in 2003, the General had transformed into the undisputed leader of the party (PDP), which then claimed to be the largest party in Africa. He had indeed become a veritable emperor.

With the party and executive power solidly behind him, the Emperor began to fish out and torment opposition within and outside the party (PDP). The EFCC that had started on a good note was turned into a ruthless war machine against the opposition, real or imagined especially after the failure of the Third Term option. In fairness to the EFCC boss, he initially seemed to have been a fearless leader—the type needed to get the job done but was unable to resist the ambition of the Emperor.

In pursuit of his uncoordinated ambition, the Emperor beamed his searchlight on his vice president who had helped him win the party primaries in the 2003 party (PDP) convention. The fight between the Emperor and his vice president consumed the whole nation and brought the operations of government to a standstill. Both the party (PDP) and government functionaries were divided along the lines of the dueling duo. Whosoever was not in support of the Emperor was seen as a supporter of the vice president and was treated with disdain. The sycophants had a field day fueling the dispute.

The assault did not stop at the supporters of the vice president but was extended to everybody who exhibited independence of mind and thought. The World Bank–trained minister of finance was unceremoniously removed and reassigned, but true to her training, she did not succumb to threats and treachery like the sycophants. In due time, she resigned her subsequent appointment and proved to Nigerians that there is dignity in independence of mind. She later returned to her former job and was subsequently appointed managing director of one of the United Nation's agencies.

It was during this period that the Emperor seized the statutory allocation of Lagos state in defiance of a Supreme Court ruling to the contrary. A major determinant of the statutory allocation to states is the state's population, largely represented by the number of local governments in the state. Lagos state is reputed to be the most populous state in the nation.

Despite its huge population, which the last census put at par with Kano state, Lagos state has just about half the number of local government areas as Kano state. To correct this imbalance, Lagos state embarked upon the cre-ation of local government areas within the state.

For selfish political reasons, the Emperor would not have this and seized the statutory allocation of the state, notwithstanding its adverse consequences on the economy of the state and the sufferings of its citizenry. This action was challenged in court by the Lagos state government; the Supreme Court of Nigeria ruled in favor of Lagos state. In an unprecedented defiance to the highest court of the land, the Emperor refused to release the said allocations to the state. This was the height of the Emperor's exhibition of impunity. While all these were going on, the second-term of the Emperor was coming to an end. Under the Nigerian constitution, the president can only run for two terms, totaling eight years. The Emperor would have finished his constitutional tenure by the end of his second term. Something had to be done to keep him in power. This was the beginning of the controversial third-term option.

THE HIGH-PROFILE MURDERS

Apart from the gruesome murder of the attorney general of the federal republic, most Nigerians will remember with deep pain the heinous murder of a chieftain of the opposition party in the Niger Delta region of Nigeria and the bloody assassination of a legal practitioner and his spouse in southeastern Nigeria.

Amazingly, in all these cold blooded mur-ders, nobody has been convicted despite the status of the victims involved and the huge sums of money wasted in setting up judicial and investigative panels.

AS IF THE DAILY KILLINGS OF ORDINARY Nigerians by stray bullets of the police, armed robbers, kidnappers, and ritual murderers were not enough, the decade witnessed some of the most terrible and horrifying assassinations of highly placed Nigerians.

It started with the murder of the attorney general of the federation, who was brutally assassinated in his home by unknown gunmen. After a lengthy rigmarole by police investigators, a prominent politician was finally charged in court for the murder. While the case was still in court and the accused under detention, the unbelievable happened. The accused ran for election into the Senate of the Federal Republic of Nigeria as a candidate under the ruling party (PDP) and was declared the winner.

The Attorney General had (AG) joined the PDP-led federal government after the rigged 1999 general elections on a purported unity government platform espoused by the Emperor and was getting ready to resign from the administration in preparation for the 2003 general election. This was not a welcome development for the party (PDP) in the southwest where the AG was the party leader of the strong and grassrooted opposition party. The PDP was not ready to lose the southwest again the way it did in 1999. So the speculation as to who was behind his assas-sination was ripe.

There were other horrifying assassinations of party leaders in other parts of the country, mostly in the opposition parties, except for the heinous killing of the PDP governorship candidate in Lagos state. But most Nigerians remember with deep pain the gruesome murder of a chieftain of the opposition party in the Niger Delta region of Nigeria and the bloody assassination of a legal practitioner and his wife in the southeast.

Amazingly, in all these cold-blooded murders, nobody has been convicted despite the status of the victims involved and the huge sums of money wasted in setting up judicial and investigative panels.

THE GODFATHER
SYNDROME

—⧼இ⧽—

No state in the nation witnessed an overwhelming portion of this phenomenon as did Anambra state. This was so sad considering the historical position of Anambra state in the political development of the southeastern part of the nation.

How could this kind of abuse, impunity, lawlessness, recklessness and criminality go unpunished?

GODFATHERISM IS THE ACT OF SPONSORING the political campaign of a candidate for the sole purpose of gaining absolute control of the state's (or local government's) finances by the sponsors after the candidate the godfather sponsored had won, or should I say, successfully rigged the election.

No state in the nation witnessed an overwhelming portion of this phenomenon as did Anambra state. This was so sad, considering the historical position of Anambra state in the political development of the southeastern part of the nation. Anambra is the home state of the first president of the Federal Republic of Nigeria, the Rt. Honorable Dr.

Nnamdi Azikiwe; Dim Emeka Odimegwu Ojukwu, former head of state of the defunct Republic of Biafra; Alex Ekwueme, former vice president of the Federal Republic of Nigeria; Cardinal Arinze and Professor Chinua Achebe, world renowned literary giants; and a host of other men of timber and caliber known throughout the nation and internationally for their religious, cultural, literary, entrepreneurial, and scientific achievements.

I recall traveling by road from Lagos to Aba in the mid-1980s during one of my vacation trips to Nigeria from the United States. All through the journey, nothing surprised me positively until I approached the Niger Bridge and on the other side of the river Niger, was the sprawling city of Onitsha. This was by far, the fastest growing city in the Nation, with perhaps the exception of Lagos at that time. I could see mini-skyscrapers sprouting all through the city, even though in an uncoordinated manner. Onitsha was indeed the bustling industrial and business center of Anambra state. This sight was heartwarming, considering that most of the eastern part of the country was just recovering from the devastating Nigerian civil war.

But in the decade ending in 2009, this state had been plagued by godfatherism, starting with the tenure of Governor Mbadinuju in 1999. The reason for this is not farfetched; external interference by powerful men in government, usually at the federal level, was the driving force.

A glaring example is what happened during the short tenure of Governor Ngige. It would be recalled that the Emperor had appointed a special adviser early in his first term whose brother was a chieftain of the party (PDP) in Anambra state. This appointment and its attendant shift of power in Anambra state became overwhelming. Who will ever believe that being such a low-level adviser to a president could bring so much power and wealth to a relatively obscure family prior to the appointment?

To make matters worse, this purported chieftain of the party (PDP) with no formal education or wealth prior to the millennium year, rose to become a member of the National Board of Trustees of the party—the highest position in the PDP. His best qualification was that he is related to the Emperor by marriage, had a brother who was an adviser to the President, and above all, had the backing of a presidential fiat.

This so-called party leader then consolidated his new position with the backing of his brother who, by then, had become a power broker at the federal level. One would have expected the brother in his advisory capacity to the Emperor to be different from the pack of political sycophants, considering his formal training and exposure in the United States of America. But no, as critics alleged, he gave both financial and political backing to his brother in the committing of atrocities against the State, culminating in the abduction of a sitting state governor in Anambra state. The story was that this party chieftain had sponsored the rigging of State Governor Ngige to power. In return, Ngige was supposed to be paying huge sums of money monthly to him from the government treasury.

However, Ngige, on becoming governor, failed to honor this illegal contract. To enforce the contract, the governor was abducted, falsely imprisoned, and in the process, compelled to sign his resignation letter before his eventual release. The independent-minded Ngige, with the support of the Anambrarians would later overcame the awesome power and impunity of the two brothers.

In retaliation, there was massive destruction of government property throughout the state by the cronies of the brothers; yet no arrest was made with respect to the governor's kidnapping or the destruction of government property worth millions of Naira. In fact, the General (President of Nigeria) would confess in a television interview that he was aware of the facts expressed above in the Ngige saga and his personal effort to settle the rift between Ngige and the purported party leader, but eventually he did nothing. This is a clear manifestation of the impunity level in the country. How could this kind of abuse, impunity, lawlessness, recklessness, and criminality go unpunished? Fortunately, we witnessed a positive departure from this political barbarism and exploitation in Anambra state with the election of Peter Obi as governor.

THE CELEBRATED TRIALS

—⟞⟡⟠⟨—

Despite the billions of Naira stolen by this governor, the embarrassment he brought to the Nigerian nation and the huge cost involved in prosecuting him, the governor was sentenced to less than two years in prison, most of which he had already spent awaiting trial.

In all these trials, millions of Naira were spent, and no strong message was passed on to the corrupt public officers or to the general public, who saw the trials and sentencing as a charade.

IN ORDER TO PROVE TO NIGERIANS AND THE the World at large that he was still fighting corruption, the Emperor and the EFCC had to create "scape-goats" among the corrupt officials. I have used the word scape goat here because of the general believe that most of the trials were incomplete and no adequate punishment was meted out even to those accused that were eventually found guilty.

The first was a former governor of a state in the Niger Delta, who had fallen out of favor with the Emperor due to his stand on the marginalization of the Niger Delta in the scheme of things. With the assistance of the EFCC, the State House of Assembly hurriedly impeached the governor on corruption charges. But before then, while the governor was abroad on medical treatment to tuck his overgrown stomach, he was arrested in transit in London and charged for money laundering.

While awaiting trial there, the then governor, jumped bail and headed for Nigeria. It was alleged that the governor had disguised himself as a woman and escaped the watchful eyes of the Metropolitan Police in London. Safely back in Nigeria, the governor went back to occupy his seat as the governor of the state in defiance of the public outcry for his unbecoming behavior. This was what prompted the EFCC to instigate, under threat, the members of the State House of Assembly to impeach him.

Despite the billions of Naira stolen by this governor, the embarrassment he brought to the Nigerian nation and the huge cost involved in prosecuting him, he was sen-tenced to less than two years in prison, most of which he had already spent awaiting trial. Thus, in a matter of weeks after the sentencing, the ex-governor was back in his mansion as a leader of his people, whom he had impoverished, still enjoying his loot.

The next scapegoat was the Inspector General of police (IG), a massively built officer. This corrupt officer was alleged to have stolen huge sums of public funds estimated at over 750 billion Naira. In the trial that ensued, the prosecution traced these billions of Naira to bank accounts in his name and those of his cronies. The amount of money involved was enough to fund a total upgrade of the entire Nigerian police force and turn it to a modern well-equipped force. Again, at the end of the trial, the former IG was sentenced to few months of imprisonment and asked to forfeit only a portion of the stolen funds. He has since been released from prison to enjoy his loot.

The last of the celebrated trials involved a former Senate president who had fallen out of favor with the Emperor. He was accused of receiving gratification for his vote in the Senate in order to pass the budget of one of the federal ministries. The only clear achievement of this trumped-up charge was his replacement as the Senate president. Nothing else was heard again about the charges as the case was never concluded.

In all these trials, millions of Naira were spent, and no strong message was passed to the corrupt public officers or to the general public, who saw the trials and sentencing as a charade. Today, so many of these cases have gone the way of indefinite abeyance.

THE THIRD-TERM OPTION

I remember vividly watching the debate on AIT Television network when the Senate president raised the gavel to rule on the option. He said, "Those in favor of the option, say yes," but the floor was silent. Nobody said a word. The Senate president once again said, "For the avoidance of doubt, those in favor, say yes." Again, the Senate floor was silent.

He then said "those against the option say nay"; there was a thunderous noise on the floor of the Senate and with that, the gavel came down. It was like a miracle: both the supporters and the opposition were in a joyous mood never witnessed on the floor of the Senate Chambers before.

AS EARLIER STATED, TOWARDS THE END OF THE Emperor's second term, the political sycophants had gone back to the drawing board on how to keep the Emperor in power beyond the constitutionally allowed tenure. What did they come up with this time? Amend the constitution to enable the Emperor run for an election the third time. From the beginning, they realized that it would not be easy to accomplish this feat.

The strategy was to organize a constitutional reform and cleverly insert the third-term option therein; this reform would encompass other pressing amendments to the constitution required for the smooth operation of government.

To achieve this, the Emperor would need to spend a lot of money by way of inducement. As for the diehard opposition, they would have to be whipped into conformity. Billions of Naira were spent organizing the constitutional amendment jamborees throughout the nation. Governors, state and federal legislators, government and nongovern-mental agencies, and other stakeholders were induced to support the option. Members of the opposition were ceaselessly harassed, detained, and charged to court on frivo-lous grounds. On several occasions, the opposition was denied the right to assemble in public places to discuss and further their positions, but they persisted, notwithstanding the threat to their lives and families.

When it seemed everything was set for the Emperor to have his way on the third-term option, the worst happened for him on the floor of the Senate. The debate on the third-term option had been on television all through despite the adverse consequences to AIT, the television company that blazed the trail to air the debate on the floor of the Senate. During the debate, the yeas and nays on the option had been evenly distributed among members of the Senate. One of the most celebrated speeches on the floor of the Senate was made by a former Senate president who had previously lost favor with the Emperor and was then facing charges of bribery and corruption. His speech was very simple and unlike what Nigerians were used to hearing from their representatives. The Senator said in effect that "if left to himself, he would have supported the option, but that his people had mandated him to vote no on the option. The speech was so dramatized that some TV stations used it as a source of attraction on their political programs long after the incident.

But the hero of the third-term option arguably was the Senate president at the time, who had consistently made his position clear on the issue, despite the adverse consequences to his political career. I vividly remember watching the debate on AIT Television network when the Senate president raised the gavel to rule on the option. He said, "Those in favor of the option say yes," and the floor was silent. Nobody said a word. The Senate president once again said "For the avoidance of doubt, those in favor, say yes." Again the Senate floor was silent. He then said "those against the option say nay." There was a thunderous noise on the floor of the Senate, and with that, the gavel came down.

It was like a miracle. Both the supporters and the opposition were in a joyous mood never witnessed on the floor of the Senate chambers before. That singular act saved the nation from the tyranny of the Emperor.

THE IMPOSITION OF A CANDIDATE

⥱〰〰⥲

In less than forty-eight hours to the election of the presidential candidate at the PDP national convention, the Emperor struck. As the Emperor that he was, he had issued a verbal decree, saying that a consensus candidate had been selected for the party and that all other candidates should step down.

However, there were some "diehards" who would not succumb to the orders of the Emperor and went ahead to contest the party primaries against the Emperor's candidate. One of such independent-minded men was a retired commodore of the Nigerian navy, a former chief of general staff, a fine officer and a gentleman, who had shown strength of character, discipline, and integrity during his career in the navy and even more now in retirement.

THE EMPEROR HAD LOST THE BATTLE FOR THE third-term but was not finished with Nigerians. By his unforgiving nature, he had to find a way to get back at Nigerians for not supporting his third-term option and still doggedly hold on to the reins of power. That opportunity came at the PDP convention to select a presidential candidate for the party in the coming 2007 general election.

Initially, the position was open to everybody who was qualified under the constitution and the guidelines of the party. Therefore, a lot of candidates trooped out in anticipation of running the race on a level playing ground. This was never to be. No wonder a lot of commentators on the party convention referred to what happened there as a selection and not an election.

Serving governors and other notable men of achieve-ment came out for the race. Most had spent huge sums of money, campaigning throughout the nation and selling their ideas of a better Nigeria. One of these candidates was the young governor of Cross River state in the Niger Delta, who had achieved a level of success in transforming his state from a relatively backward state to a modern one, especially the capital city of Calabar. In his eight years in power, this governor built one of the best export-pro-cessing zones in Africa in his state capital, cleaned up the environment, and made the state the number-one tourist destination in Nigeria.

I was shocked when last I visited the state to find out that the modern export processing zone (EPZ)/TINAPA built in Calabar with huge resources generated from the coffers of the state and private equity contribution was wasting because of the political considerations of some political sycophants within the federal government. What kind of federal government would block such huge inflow of foreign investment and the attendant benefits to the masses, the people of the state and Nigerians in general, based on petty, selfish, political considerations?

In less than forty-eight hours to the election of the presidential candidate at the PDP national convention, the Emperor struck. As the emperor that he was, he had issued a verbal decree that a consensus candidate had been selected for the party and that all other candidates should step down. There were pockets of protest, but the Emperor had spoken. This pronouncement effectively wiped out most of the best candidates from the race.

However, there were some diehards, who would not succumb to the orders of the Emperor and went ahead to contest the party primaries against the Emperor's candidate. One of such independent-minded men was a retired commodore of the Nigerian Navy, who was the Chief of General Staff under the Ibrahim Babangida military regime. He is a fine officer and a gentleman, who had shown strength of character, discipline, and integrity during his career in the navy and even more now in retirement.

The result of the election was obvious. During the counting of the ballot papers after the voting at the PDP national convention, the name Umoru dominated over 90 percent of the votes cast.

I felt pity for my very good friend who had to stand several hours in the cold night of the federal capital city, Abuja, to witness the counting session of this charade called an election as a representative of one of the candidates that I had earlier described. It was alleged by critics that a lot of money had exchanged hands in the night preceding the voting; resulting in this quasi-election, which was a total show of shame and selection of a candidate against the will of the people.

THE ELECTION OF 2007

The apathy to the campaign trails from the fact that the voters already knew that their votes were not going to make a difference in the outcome of the election. This was because the Emperor had declared the election to be "a do or die affair," and since the majority of the people were not ready to die for nothing, the apathy grew.

To disprove the increasing conviction that the candidate had died while receiving med-ical treatment abroad, the Emperor in one of the campaign rallies placed an interna-tional telephone call to the candidate and asked the now infamous question, "Umoru, are you dead?" He continued, "Please tell Nigerians that you are still alive."

There were other incidents of mockery of our democratic process as exemplified in other states in the southeast and southwest where candidates in jail on corruption/murder charges went ahead to win elections in absentia as state governor and senator of the Federal Republic

*of Nigeria, respectively. What a country! These
kinds of unbelievable stories could only be told
or happen in Nigeria.*

HAVING SUCCESSFULLY SELECTED THE presidential candidate for the PDP, it was time to sell the candidate to the entire nation. The PDP campaign for the 2007 general election was a massive build-up of party stalwarts headed by the Emperor who had now left his primary function as President to become the de facto campaign manager of the PDP presidential candidate.

The PDP campaign train moved from city to city and state to state, trying to sell their candidate to unwilling docile voters. The apathy to the campaign stemmed from the fact that the voters already knew that their votes were not going to make a difference in the outcome of the election. This was so because the Emperor had declared the election to be "a do or die affair," and since the majority of the people were not ready to die for nothing, the apathy grew.

The frail PDP candidate was little known throughout the nation even though he had been a governor of one of the northern states. There were rumors of his failing health. The rumors became facts when the candidate could not consistently campaign for more than one month in a row without seeking medical attention overseas. In one of his campaign rallies, he was alleged to have collapsed and had to be rushed to a hospital abroad.

To disprove the increasing conviction that the candidate had died while receiving medical treatment abroad, the Emperor in one of the campaign rallies placed an international telephone call to the candidate and asked the now infamous question, "Umoru, are you dead?" He continued,

"Please tell Nigerians that you are still alive." This telephone conversation was going on from a podium in a cam-paign rally in full view of the crowd and people watching on television all over the nation. This was the height of mockery of our democracy as this candidate would later be declared the winner in the general election.

There were other incidents of mockery of our democratic process as exemplified in other states in the southeast and southwest where candidates in jail on corruption or murder charges went ahead to win elections in absentia as state governor and senator of the Federal Republic of Nigeria, respectively. What a country? These kinds of unbelievable stories could only be told in Nigeria.

If the 2003 election was adjudged substantially rigged by both local and international observers, the 2007 general elections would go down in history as the worst election ever conducted in the history of the nation and the world over.

There was violence everywhere, and ballot papers were not serialized as required by the electoral guidelines and were flown in from another African country just a day or so before the election. It was generally alleged that ballot papers were massively thumb-printed in the houses of party stalwarts and officially escorted to the collation centers. Thumb-printed ballot papers presumably from polling booths were discarded, destroyed, and thrown by the way-sides. It was a shame and a mockery of what could in any way be called an election.

Everybody condemned the conduct of the election with the exception of the PDP and some pockets of other riggers in some parts of the nation. The election tribunals set up to hear cases arising from the election would overturn a lot of the election results at the state and federal levels.

Unfortunately, some of the cases lingered longer in courts, especially in the southwest part of the country, two years after the election. It was a clear case of "judgment delayed equals judgment denied."

In one of the southwestern states, a rerun election was held after two years of the election. Yet the conduct of the rerun election was more disturbing and a shameless exhibition of electoral abuse, so much so that the chief electoral officer of the state publicly denounced the conduct and the collation process of the election. She stated that announcing the result of the massively rigged election as approved by the Independent National Electoral Commission (INEC) would be against her conscience. However, after several days of threats to her life, she was compelled to announce the result contrary to her conscience. Soon thereafter, the rerun election result and the aggrieved candidate were back in the electoral tribunal.

The most painful and hopeless part of this episode was that the Supreme Court of Nigeria in a split decision, affirmed the election of the PDP presidential candidate despite massive evidence to the contrary. Once again, our quasi-democracy was raped, and the rapists were set scot free by the highest court of the nation. The sycophants' slogan, "Let's give peace and our nascent democracy a chance," once again reigned.

THE ELECTORAL REFORMS

—◦◦◦—

During the presentation of the committee's report, the president thanked the members and praised them for the thorough job they did on the national assignment and prom-ised speedy implementation.

We were approaching another general election, and yet the president's inaugural promise on electoral reforms was still in the cooler. This was happening despite the huge sums of money spent in producing the committee's report, including a nationwide tour by members of the committee and the increasing public outcry in support of a speedy passage of the report in its original form.

THE NEW PRESIDENT, WHO HAD CAPTURED the mandate of the people, was sworn-in at a colorful inauguration celebration. During his inaugural speech, the president acknowledged the flaws in the 2007 general election and promised an electoral reform that would guard against the sort of election that brought him to power. The promise was a welcome relief for many Nigerians who were fast losing hope in our collective ability to do things right. True to his promise, the new president set up the Electoral Reform Committee headed by a former chief justice of the Supreme Court.

The composition of the committee had other eminent jurists, members of professional bodies, organized labor, bankers, the business community, and men and women of outstanding quality in the society. Even the critics gave the president kudos for keeping his promise and applauded the composition of the committee.

These men of integrity would go to work for several months and come up with what they believed was a dependable way forward in our electoral process. Their recommendations were far-reaching, touching on all aspects of the electoral process, including the procedure for the appointment of the chairman of the Independent National Electoral Commission (INEC). The committee had reasoned that for there to be a positive change in our electoral process, the word *independent* in the name of the commission must be resurrected and made real.

During the presentation of the Committee's report, the president thanked the members and praised them for the thorough job they did on the national assignment and promised speedy implementation. But the political sycophants in the presidency would not agree to not having the important position of INEC chairman under the total control of the president. Consequently, the president was convinced to appoint another three-man committee within his cabinet headed by the Attorney General of the federation to review the work of the committee.

Of course, the sycophants had their way and would argue that the committee's recommendation on the appointment of the chairman of INEC would conflict with the constitutional provision on separation of powers.

However, such an argument is inconsequential as critics likened it to the appointment of the Chief Justice/Justices of the Supreme Court by the President with the consent of the Senate without creating any conflict in our constitutional provision of separation of powers.

While the arguments raged, we were approaching another general election without the fulfillment of the President's inaugural promise on electoral reforms. The National Assembly, which is empowered to make laws for the good governance of the nation, has been in limbo and did nothing for several months just like in every other major bill of importance to the nation that has been presented on the floor of the two chambers including the freedom of the press bill.

This was happening despite the huge sums of money spent in producing the committee's report, including a nationwide tour by members of the committee and the increasing public outcry in support of speedy passage of the report in its original form.

THE SEVEN-POINT AGENDA AND THE 202020 VISION

———◈◈◈———

This 202020 vision proposes to make Nigeria one of the top twenty economies in the world by the year 2020. It was a very ambitious program for a nation that is lacking and deficient in every aspect of our national development, with no functional infrastructures, health care, or educational system and with an unemployment level approaching 40 percent and a poverty level that is unprecedented in the history of any country with our kind of abundance of material resources and human endowments.

This is the state of a nation that would become one of the twenty biggest econ-omies in the world in less than ten years from then. That would be the ninth wonder of the world.

DURING HIS ELECTION CAMPAIGN, THE president had made the 202020 Vision the cardinal point of his administration. This 202020 vision proposed to make Nigeria one of the top twenty economies in the world by the year 2020. It was a very ambitious program for a nation that is lacking and deficient in every aspect of nation development, with no infrastructures (roads, railroads, electricity) as homes and businesses struggled to provide their own electricity through power generating sets, which had turned the whole nation into a gigantic factory powered by generating sets. There was no healthcare system as the hospitals had been turned to death traps where morticians made more money than surgeons and other medical practitioners.

The nation had no functional educational system, as our ivory towers had become a breeding ground for gangs and prostitutes worse than the biblical story of Sodom and Gomorrah.

Unemployment was approaching 40 percent, with a poverty level that was unprecedented in the history of any country of this size and blessed with an abundance of material resources and human endowments.

Greed, sycophancy, and poverty of the mind had turned our citizenry into a docile lot, willingly accepting the atrocities of their leaders who went unpunished.

This was the state of the nation that would become one of the twenty biggest economies in the world in 2020—that is, in less than ten years. That would be the ninth wonder of the world.

How would the President achieve this laudable audacious goal or would it go like the Vision 2010? The pres-ident came up with a seven-point agenda that included among others, focus on massive building and rebuilding of infrastructures, electric power generation, education, agriculture, and so forth. But what has happened so far is all talk, more talk, and no action; just like the Vision 2010, which had come and gone without any recorded success.

However, there were some recorded improvements in infrastructural developments in some states of the nation like Lagos, Cross River, Akwa Ibom, Enugu, Kwara, and a few other states. I have mentioned these states here because of the positive leadership examples shown by the state governors therein, especially in Lagos state where the governor is doing such a fabulous job of assisting Lagos to regain its pride of place as the city of excellence and a mega city to be reckoned with in Africa.

However, for the rest of the nation, for almost six months, the educational system ground to a halt as the teachers' associations of all tertiary institutions in the nation went on strike to press for better working conditions. While the strike was on, it was rumored that the minister of education spent over 50 million Naira on a birthday party, a colossal waste of public funds that angered the striking workers even more.

In the power sector, the total number of megawatts available to the nation remained the same or even dropped from where it was two years previously when the President was sworn in. In most parts of the country, you were lucky if you got up to a total of two hours of electricity supply in a twenty-four-hour period. The colossal amount of funds already invested in this power sector without any significant progress led the House of Representatives to probe the sector. The story is the same for all the sectors, which were the focal point of the seven-point agenda of Mr. President. No wonder a lot of commentators advised the president to cut his agenda to two points and stop dissipating energy on all seven points without a tangible result in any sector.

Yet no single notable individual has been convicted of any wrongdoing in the power sector scandal in the past two years even as a scapegoat, like in the days of the Emperor.

The reason for this is because the president tried to cover his inability to take effective action against these alleged state fraudsters and evil men of our nation by hiding under the rule of law/due process policy of his administration; a *sine qua non* for ineffectiveness, especially against corrupt public officers as we have seen nations with effective rule of law in place still indict and convict public officers who abuse their privileged positions..

Indeed during this era, rule of law was tantamount to not enforcing the law. Otherwise, how does one explain the inability of our system to convict accused ex-governors when there is incontrovertible evidence against them with respect to billions of Naira of public funds transferred from their states' statutory accounts to their private business accounts?

THE EFCC ANGLE

———◦◦◦———

The hunter has now become the hunted.

The prosecution of the ex-governors who had been charged with looting the treasury of their various states was put in abeyance for one reason or the other.

People would not effectively discharge their functions when they were unsure of being protected by the system that they worked for or that criminal acts would be prosecuted.

This is one of the reasons why our nation finds it difficult to develop. There is so much impunity and uncertainty in our policy trust.

THE ADMINISTRATION OF THE PRESIDENT started with the controversy over which department of the administration would be in charge of prosecuting the corrupt officials, especially the governors. After lengthy hassling between the Attorney General (AG) of the federation and the EFCC, the sycophants had the day. The responsibility of prosecuting the corrupt officials rested mostly with the AG and rightly so. But what has happened since then can only be imagined.

As the custodian of the government's new initiative of the rule of law and due process policy, the AG would grind everything to a halt. The prosecution of the ex-governors who had been charged with looting the treasury of their various states was put in abeyance for one reason or the other. Part of the reason given for the slow pace of prosecution was missing files. How can case files be missing in the custody of officers charged with safeguarding the said files? Why has no officer of the agency been charged for destroying evidence? Even if the files are lost, these are financial crimes committed through the banks. Why did the agency not go back to the primary sources in the various banks to obtain secondary copies?

Answers to these questions would go a long way in proving the unwillingness of the administration to prosecute these cases to a logical conclusion. To make matters worse, the government beamed its searchlight on the ex-boss of the EFCC. The hunter had now become the hunted. He was first demoted in rank, was disgraced during the graduation ceremony of the School of Strategic Studies (where he had been sent after his removal from office), and then charged in court for corruption. The reason for his persecution is not farfetched. The ex-EFCC boss had relentlessly tried to bring the corrupt ex-governors to justice or so it seemed.

Critics were of the view that some of the powerful and corrupt ex-governors who had funded the president's campaign were responsible for the appointment of the AG. Therefore, it was not in the AG's self-interest to go against his masters; in other words, he was put there to do the bidding of his masters, period. From the inception of the new administration, the former EFCC boss had known no peace. The question is, how do you expect the current EFCC boss to go ahead and do her job without fear or favor, knowing what might befall her at the expiration of her tenure or with a change in government?

This is one of the reasons why our nation is slow in development. There is so much impunity and uncertainty in our policy trust. People will not effectively discharge their functions when they are unsure of being protected by the system that they work for or that criminal acts would be prosecuted.

THE TRIALS OF THE EX-GOVERNORS

—◦◦◦—

While the court was in session, there was a mammoth crowd outside in colorful uniforms of native attire singing, chanting, and praising this ex-governor who was being tried for looting several billions of Naira of public funds and thereby rendering his state and its people underdeveloped and poor. Ironically, it's this same people who have been robbed that are now wearing uniforms, standing in the rain and praising this alleged shameless criminal.

To add insult to injury, when the court session was over, this alleged looter of public funds came to the cheering arms of this perverse crowd and spent over fifteen minutes addressing the press on how government should tackle the issue of world hunger, a topical issue then, before he hopped into his brand-new SUV and drove off. I was shocked and sad for my people.

What kind of people are these? I imagined. This is beyond poverty. It's a peculiar kind of poverty, a poverty of the mind, the worst kind of disease that could befall a nation.

> *How do we effectively fight corruption when the*
> *current governors can see that no punishment*
> *had been meted out to their predecessors for*
> *financial crimes committed against their*
> *various states? Until we begin to punish*
> *our public officers for wrongful acts against*
> *the State, we will never have sustainable*
> *development in our nation.*

WITH THE NEW AG FIRMLY IN CHARGE, THE trials of the ex-governors almost ground to halt. The reason for this has already been explained in the previous chapter. Our focus here is to look deeper at the sycophantic side of our people and the inefficiency of our systems.

I remember watching one of the court sessions in Lagos during the trial of one of the ex-governors from one of the southeastern states. While the court was in session, there was a mammoth crowd outside in colorful uniforms made of native attires singing, chanting, and praising this ex-governor who was being tried for looting several billions of naira from the state treasury, thereby rendering his state and its people underdeveloped and poor.

Ironically, it's this same people who have been robbed that were now wearing uniforms, standing in the rain and praising this shameless alleged criminal who had moved from a rented three-bedroom apartment just prior to his election as a governor to owning most of the posh properties and other businesses in his state with billions of Naira in his bank accounts.

What kind of people are these? I imagined. This is beyond poverty. It's a peculiar kind of poverty; a poverty of the mind, the worst kind of disease that could befall a nation.

To add insult to injury, when the court session was over, this alleged looter of public funds came to the cheering arms of this perverse crowd and spent over fifteen minutes addressing the press on how government should tackle the issue of world hunger, a topical issue then, before he hopped into his brand-new SUV and drove off. I was shocked and sad for my people. Again, I asked myself what kind of a people is this?

In other civilized countries or even not so civilized, a man standing trial for looting state funds would cover his face in shame and would hurriedly get into his car to get away from the glaring view of the people whom he had destroyed. But that does not happen in Nigeria, where alleged common criminals are worshipped, revered, and have a lot of praise singers at their disposal for looting public funds.

In another trial, the accused ex-governor had the impudence in court to request the judge to grant him leave to go abroad for medical treatment. This was a public officer who had the mandate of his people to among other things develop suitable health-care facilities for his state during his tenure as the governor. Instead, the ex-governor allegedly converted huge sums of the state's funds into his personal accounts to the detriment of the developmental projects in his state. Today in court, he is asking the judge to grant him leave to go and spend the alleged stolen state funds abroad on medical treatment when the people of his state are dying of hunger and disease at home.

A similar case was the celebrated corruption trial of a former governor of one of the states in the Niger Delta. This ex-governor was first arraigned on a 170-count corruption charge, involving N9.2bn, at the Federal High Court (FHC) but successfully challenged the jurisdiction of the court at the appeals court, having lost at the high court.

The court of appeal ruled that criminal cases must be tried in the division of the Federal High Court that was nearest to the venue where the crime was committed. In line with the judgment, the case was reassigned to FHC, Asaba, where a judge quashed the charges against the former governor for "want of evidence."

The EFCC appealed the judgment and went ahead to press fresh charges against the embattled ex-governor following a petition by the elders and stakeholders forum of his home state, the Ex-Governor was granted bail. Thereafter, he fled to the

United Arab Emirates, where his extradition was being processed. He would later be arrested, tried, and sentenced in London for money laundry.

Another case involving a former governor of a state in the southwest is ironic, considering the reasons given by his counsel for prolonging the trial. The ex-governor is standing trial on a fifty-one-count corruption charge involving N1.2bn; the case has dragged since 2006 while the ex-governor is on bail on health grounds.

The ex-governor had approached the court with the complaint that he no longer had the "financial wherewithal to further defray accommodation and transportation bills" to attend court sessions during the hearing of his case with the EFCC. This, coming from a man accused of embezzling public funds in excess of N1 billion, is totally absurd.

Yet some other ex-governors were able to obtain court injunctions against State prosecution for crimes committed against the State. What kind of a system would grant immunity against trial to a government official for financial crimes committed against the State and its people and still within the statutes of limitation?

How do we effectively fight corruption when the current Governors can see that no punishment had been meted out to their predecessors for financial crimes committed against their various states? Until we begin to punish our public officers for wrongful acts against the State, we will never have sustainable development in our nation.

THE HOUSE OF REPRESENTATIVES POWER PROBE

─୰୰─

In the company of TV Cameras, the House of Representatives Power Committee members led by its chairman headed to the sites. What they saw in the full view of all Nigerians will clearly illustrate why the country appears to be doomed.

From one site to the other, the story was the same. The contractors had just taken the monies and gone on a globetrotting spending spree. In full glare of television cameras, members of the committee asked the contractors the following questions at their sites: How much was the contract sum? How much has been disbursed, and what is the level of work done so far?

In most cases, the only visible work done on the sites were the erection of signboards of the companies and some fencing on the portion of the land earmarked for the projects. On some other sites, the committee members were shown shipping documents evidencing importation of the materials for the job nearly two years after disbursement of funds to the contractors.

After the drama at the construction sites of these contractors nationwide, it was time for the committee to go back and report their findings to the full House of Representatives. If Nigerians were shocked at the site visits, they were more saddened by what happened on the floor of the House of Representatives.

What a colossal waste of the Nation's financial resources allegedly totaling over 15 billion USD!

POWER OUTRAGES IN NIGERIA IS A MAJOR reason businesses are failing or performing at a level below optimum. "God at creation said, 'Let there be light' and there was light." In Nigeria, the government decided that the people should live in darkness, and consequently, Nigeria holds the world record for the importation of electric power generators. Until power generation is taken care of, the prohibitive cost of production will continue to be a disincentive to business growth.

In the words of Professor Barth Nnaji, an acclaimed authority in this field: "Many other countries who were at relatively the same level with Nigeria in the 1960s and early 1970s have found themselves at ten times more than Nigeria's installed capacity today. In Africa, South Africa, with a population of 45 million people, has an installed capacity of 46,000 Megawatts. Even Ghana with a population of 21 million people has an installed capacity of 1,800 MW. I was shocked when the president of Zambia told me last week that they have an installed capacity of 2,000 MW for a population of 11 million and want to grow its power generation to 8,000 MW."

Now Nigeria, with a population of over 150 million people, can only boast of an installed capacity of 4,000 MW. This is a paradoxical figure. Perhaps even more startling figures would be the per capita power capacity measured in watts per person. For the United States, it is 2,900 watts per person. South Africa is 1,050 watts per person; Brazil is 480; India is 110, Zambia is 181 watts per person, and even Ghana is 85 watts per person, but Nigeria is 29 watts per person, which is not even enough to light a bulb not to mention an industrial machine.

Prompted by the massive outcry caused by the increasing deterioration of electricity supply, thereby plunging the nation into total darkness, the power committee in the House of Representatives decided to probe the power sector in the exercise of its oversight functions.

It was reported in the press that between 6 to 15 billion USD had been spent on the power sector within the eight years of the Emperor's reign as the president of the Federal Republic of Nigeria. The emperor acknowledged spending about 6 billion USD (against the 15 billion USD alleged by other sources) on the power sector during the period. Even with that huge expenditure, the total megawatts of electricity generated for the entire nation had dropped from about 3,000 megawatts in 1999 to less than that figure in 2009. After listening to testimonies during the committee hearings, which the Emperor declined to attend in person, it was time for visits to the sites of these multibillion Naira contracts by members of the committee. It is an understatement to say that Nigerians were shocked at the outcome of the visits. In the company of TV cameras, the committee members led by its chairman headed for the sites. What they saw in the full view of all Nigerians clearly illustrates why the country seems doomed.

From one site to the other, the story was the same. The contractors had just taken the monies and gone on globetrotting spending sprees. In the full glare of television cameras, members of the committee asked the contractors the following questions at their sites, "How much was the contract sum? How much has been disbursed to you, and what is the level of work you have done so far? In most cases, the only visible work done on the sites were the erection of signboards of the contractors and some fencing on the portion of the land earmarked for the projects. On some other sites, members of the committee were shown some shipping documents evidencing shipment of the materials required to do the job nearly two years after disbursement of funds to the contractors. It was a pitiful sight for the contractors, members of the committee, and the general public, watching the unfolding drama on their television sets nationwide.

After the drama at the construction sites of these contractors nationwide, it was time for the committee to go back and report their findings to the full House of Representatives. If Nigerians were shocked at the result of the site visits, they were more saddened by what happened on the floor of the House of Representatives.

There arose a disagreement among members of the committee as to the contents of the report. For whatever reason, the individual members of the committee could no longer agree on what every Nigerian saw on televisions sets during the site visits. Some commentators had alleged that huge sums of money had exchanged hands in the process of writing the committee report hence, the disagreement among members. This disagreement delayed the official presentation of the report on the floor of the House of Representatives to date.

Although it was proved beyond doubt that contracts were awarded without due process, that huge sums of money running into billions of USD were disbursed, and that no tangible work was done at the contract sites, no contractor has been arrested or charged in court.

Ironically, the only victim of the power probe was the chairman of the power committee in the House of Representatives who had warmed himself to the hearts of many Nigerians in his steadfast approach to the power probe. The question on the lips of many Nigerians was, why would a man with so much promise simply destroy himself for money? The chairman of the house committee on power was arrested and charged with corruption. It was alleged that he was involved in a fraudulent financial scandal involving a huge sum of money earmarked for the power sector.

He had forgotten the adage that "He who lives in a glass house should not throw stones." The chairman did throw stones, and his glass mansion was subsequently shattered as a consequence. Nevertheless, a lot of Nigerians still admire him for "throwing the stones." What a colossal waste of the nation's financial resources allegedly totaling over 15 billion USD.

NIGERIAN NATIONAL PETROLEUM CORPORATION (NNPC) AND THE BLACK GOLD

Prior to the discovery of crude oil (black gold) in Nigeria in the late 1950s, the economy of the nation was growing steadily and was acclaimed to be the fastest-growing in sub-Saharan Africa. It would have been expected that, with the discovery of oil, things would just get a lot better as it has in other nations so endowed. But that was not the case in Nigeria.

How can a nation that prides itself on being the World sixth-largest producer of crude oil not be able to refine the same crude for the benefit of its people?

The reason is very simple: the sycophants in government along with their cronies have long realized that fixing the refineries would foreclose their easy access to milking public funds. Consequently, the refineries must stay

> *down despite the billions of naira regularly spent on the turnaround maintenance (TAM) of the said refineries.*
>
> *The NNPC along with the defunct Nigerian Airways, NIPOST, and NEPA, has consistently topped the corruption chart in the public sector of the nation. The level of waste and corruption in the NNPC is incomparable to that of any other national company of its size and endowment.*

IT IS AN UNDISPUTED FACT THAT NIGERIA RANKS very low in the world when you compare its natural and human resources with its level of development and the suffering of its people. The reason for this sorrowful state of our nation is not farfetched.

Prior to the discovery of crude oil (black gold) in Nigeria in the late 1950s, the economy of the nation was growing steadily. The rate of growth was the fastest-growing in sub-Saharan Africa. Education, health, and living standards of the people were very high. Graduates were able to secure jobs upon graduation; electricity and water supply were very steady though limited in area of coverage but growing; and our educational standard was one of the highest in the continent of Africa. Agriculture was the mainstay of our economy, and Nigerians were successful in the cultivation of the major cash crops that earned them much foreign exchange; there was security of life and property and availability of other good things that made life worth living.

It was expected that with the discovery of oil, things would have become a lot better as it has in other nations so endowed. But that was not the case as Nigerians are all aware of the negative impact that the discovery of the black gold had brought to the nation. Our development and gross domestic product (GDP) have been on the decline comparatively despite the huge sums of foreign exchange raked in yearly from the sale of our crude oil.

With the exception of the period before and soon after the Nigerian civil war when there was massive reconstruction of infrastructure, the country has never witnessed any meaningful development again.

The government agency charged with the management of this number-one world commodity (black gold) is the Nigerian National Petroleum Corporation (NNPC). This agency along with the defunct Nigerian Airways, Nigerian Postal Services (NIPOST), and National Electric Power Authority (NEPA), has consistently topped the corruption chart in the public sector of the nation. The level of waste and corruption in the NNPC is incomparable to that of any other national company of its size and endowment.

A review of the official website indicates that within a space of ten months between 2003 and 2004, the Revenue Mobilization Allocation and Fiscal Commission (RMAFC) and the National Assembly openly contested the accounting methods of the NNPC, alleging grave irreg-ularities in its dealings. The RMAFC had objected vehe-mently to the NNPC's unauthorized sale of crude oil—in excess of the 450,000 barrels allocated daily for local con-sumption—and the arbitrary manner in which proceeds were converted from dollars to naira. According to the commission's petition in 2003, the NNPC disposed of hundreds of thousands of barrels daily at $32 per barrel, while declaring $18 for purposes of remittance to the federation account.

In October 2004, for instance, NNPC's remittances to the federation account were converted at an exchange rate of N131.88 to the United States dollar, while a rate of N132.38 to the dollar was used for the joint venture (JV) account as well as the excess crude account. In clear monetary terms, the RMAFC had put resultant losses that year alone at N300 billion, being "the excess amount that was not paid into the federation account."

The NNPC's sharp practices have continued to date. Yet the presidency did not take appropriate action against the management of the NNPC. The documentation of irregularities and the many channels used by the RMAFC to publicize the rip-off by key officials of the NNPC and the CBN has not moved the federal government to check the trend.

The presidency, which directly controls the ministry of petroleum resources, has continued to allocate to the corporation 450,000 barrels of crude oil per day, when it is unable to process half of that quantity of crude oil. It is common knowledge that the indifference of the presi-dency has fostered a culture of corruption and impunity, as was evidenced by the NNPC's refusal to pay into the federation account proceeds from crude oil allocated for domestic consumption, and its preference to sell it at the international market between 1999 and 2007.

The National Assembly in exercise of its oversight functions should unearth the NNPC's diverse sources of revenue and how these have been managed over the years, especially since 1999. A forensic audit of the accounts and operations of the corporation has become necessary and urgent.

While the negative impact of this mismanagement is well known to Nigerians, what Nigerians don't understand is why it has been impossible in the last decade to fix the nation's four refineries and stop the colossal waste of public funds in subsidizing importation of refined petro-leum products.

How can a nation that prides itself on being the world's sixth-largest producer of crude oil not be able to refine the same crude for the benefit of its people? The reason is very simple: the sycophants in government along with their cronies have long realized that fixing the refineries would foreclose their easy access to milking public funds. Consequently the refineries must stay down despite the billions of Naira regularly spent on the turnaround maintenance (TAM) of the said refineries.

The deputy chairman of the House of Representatives Committee on Petroleum Downstream once said that the implications of the inefficiency of the NNPC on the economy cannot be ignored. In his words, "We are alarmed over the allegation of monumental corruption leveled against the NNPC and its subsidiaries, particularly the Pipeline Products Marketing Company (PPMC), to the extent that a clique in NNPC and PPMC has been receiving $500,000 then daily from a fuel importation cartel . . . to the detriment of the Nigerian state".

The House consequently summoned the group man-aging director of NNPC and the managing directors of PPMC and the PPPRA as well as the representatives of the major oil marketers association (MOMAN). However, a top trade union executive saw the probe as a wild-goose chase designed to achieve nothing, for the simple reason that members of the House of Representatives would not muster enough courage to probe the NNPC that sponsored them to a retreat in Uyo (Akwa Ibom state), even though there is an allocation for same in the House budget.

Another oil workers' trade union executive also declared that probing the NNPC is an exercise purposely designed to dance to the gallery because the lawmakers do not need to conduct a probe before sanitizing the petroleum sector for the simple fact that efficient periodic checks on the activities of the corporation and the oil industry would have detected some of these ills. So far no officer of the corporation has been arrested and charged for these allegations of corruption.

THE PRIVATE SECTOR

—❧—

How does one explain a situation where very senior public officers and other highly placed individuals convert public assets to their own private use in the name of privatization? That was substantially what happened in Transcorp PLC.

Looking at this scenario and others in the banking and stock market sectors, it is very clear that the public sector rot, abuse, impunity, fraud, and other crimes committed against the State without punishment for the wrongful acts have been effectively transferred to the private sector in Nigeria from 1999 to 2009.

The cost of diesel to run the generators was a major factor in crippling these small-scale industries. How do you compete as an entrepreneur when one item in your cost profile almost equals the total cost of your competitors elsewhere? However, if the power situation ten years ago was bad, it degenerated to its worst level in the decade under review.

The CBN intervention has exposed so many corporate malpractices and primitive accumulation of wealth by chief executives of banks whose primary responsibility it was to grow the assets of their various banks. The chief executives' quest for wealth accumulation went beyond greed; it became madness. In their quest for wealth, just like the politicians, they forgot that the world is just a transit point and not our final destination.

THIS DECADE CANNOT BE CONCLUDED without reflecting on the adverse impacts on some key sectors of our economy. The next few paragraphs will review some of these key sectors.

The manufacturing sector would probably go down as the most affected in this decade of sycophancy and waste. I recall going to the commercial city of Aba as the branch manager of a bank in 1998. I was amazed at the concentration, or should I say cluster, of small-scale industries in the Osisioma area of the city. Looking back, I could see the wisdom in locating the Alaoji Power Plant there in Aba. The industrial sector of the city was very vibrant with factories producing items ranging from plastics to table water, tissue paper, shoes, soft drinks, nails, aluminum, vegetable oil, pharmaceuticals, spare parts, palm oil and kernel oil, electrical materials, and so forth. Just name it, and it was there. No wonder, Aba became known in some quarters as "the Tokyo of Nigeria."

As a branch manager then, my duty entailed visiting these customers, finding out their needs, and helping proffer solutions to them. So I had first-hand information of the development in the area. One of the fundamental constraints of these industries then was power. Electricity supply was and is still almost nonexistent, and the factories are run day and night on generators. The cost of diesel to run the generators was a major factor in crippling these small-scale industries. The disparity in the price of diesel to petrol shows that the problem is systemic. Elsewhere in the world, the difference in the price of diesel to petrol is minimal. But in Nigeria, the reverse is the case. How do you compete as an entrepreneur when one item in your cost profile almost equals the total cost of your competitors elsewhere? This is the reason why only buying and selling thrives in most part of the country while the manufacturing sector has suffered tremendously.

Apart from the irredeemable power situation, the government policy was very adverse to the business environment. As a commercial city, Aba had relied on the proximity of the seaports in Port Harcourt and Calabar for its import and export transactions. These two ports were rendered almost inoperative by government policies in a manner that seemed to be a punishment to the people of the area. Some items like textile materials that were once sought from Aba and from all over the country ceased to be. The market has since moved.

Additionally, the security situation had become unbearable for any decent family to live with. Security of lives and property could no longer be guaranteed by the government of Abia state. A combination of these major constraints was responsible for the closing down of these small-scale industries and other business enterprises in Abia state. Consequently, the bustling city of Aba has now turned to a ghost town, a shadow of itself ten years ago. This story is the same for most industrial cities in the country as no part of the country was spared.

Another part of the private sector of the economy that was adversely affected in this decade was the financial sector. The banking subsector started off on a good note despite the criticism that trailed the banking sector consolidation. But like most things in Nigeria, the consolidation process created monsters in the new chief executives that emerged with the consolidation. Corporate governance was relegated to the background, and banks that were once regarded as big, strong, and reliable began to depend on the Central Bank of Nigeria's (CBN) expanded discount window for funding of their day-to-day transactions.

The CBN intervention exposed so many corporate malpractices and primitive accumulation of wealth by Chief Executives of banks, whose primary responsi-bility it was to grow the assets of their various banks. The Chief Executives' quest for wealth accumulation has gone beyond greed; it is now madness. In their quest for wealth, just like the politicians, they have forgotten that the world is just a transit point and not our final destination. Members of the boards of banks were merely used as rubber stamps to affirm decisions of the CEOs of banks, who specialized in financial engineering of banks' books; and bank officers who aided them were adequately rewarded by the executives. The lessons from the book titled The 1890 Banker, which taught bankers to serve and be conservative in their approach were totally lost. Bank officers were no longer encouraged to develop and grow business relationships from which proceeds of the business would naturally be channeled to the banks.

Rather, they were compelled to focus on deposit mobilization, and it did not matter the ways and means applied in getting those deposits. Bankers who were once respected persons in the society were turned to mere beggars for deposits, sometimes to the detriment of their bodies especially for the female staff. No wonder the stress level among bankers became incomparable to that of the workforce in any other sector of the economy.

The CBN invested a whopping sum of almost one trillion Naira to save the banking industry from collapse during the period. Some commentators criticized the CBN for the intervention, but imagine what would have happened if Nigerians woke up one morning to see two or three of their purportedly most capitalized banks in dis-tress and unable to meet their over-the-counter payment obligations? Certainly, there would have been widespread panic in the country with its adverse consequences on our economy.

That is why I supported the CBN intervention despite its shortcomings. Details of the root causes of the banking distress in Nigeria and the CBN intervention are available in my book titled Nemesis, published in December 2009 and summarized here: The news hit the Nigerian public like a thunderbolt. The managing directors/CEOs along with their board members of eight banks in the country were axed by the CBN.

The proximate cause of the CBN action was quite obvious to even the uninformed. What was not so obvious was the remote causes, which were an accumulation of boardroom wheeling dealing, where greed and avarice reigned. Here, only the mean, strong, influential and ruthless survive.

A major causes of the bank crisis could be traced to the 25 billion Naira minimum shareholders fund directive of the CBN, which was hurriedly concluded at the end of 2005. Most of the banks that could not meet the mandatory 25 billion Naira benchmark resorted to financial engineering to meet the dead line. This created gaps in the banks' books, coupled with their existing huge bad loan portfolios and other related unresolved merger issues.

The new CBN governor on assumption of office discovered that five of the eight affected banks had been involved in 95 percent of the transactions in the expanded discount window, which was an avenue, created by the CBN, to make ready short-term funds available to banks to settle outstanding debts backed by viable projects.

The CBN ordered a special bank audit as a result of this and found that the capital adequacy of the banks had depleted substantially, resulting in liquidity problems in the affected banks. Consequently five of the eight banks couldn't meet their daily obligations without borrowing from the CBN expanded discount window.

Second, there was an intense size-driven competition and quest for expansion among the banks in the industry without developing the capacity to manage such growth. Thus, a lot of funds were tied up in physical assets (new branches) without corresponding growth in the deposits mobilized from the new branches.

Third, the Nigerian Stock Exchange had billions of Naira in bank funds tied up in margin trading with huge loans having been given out to individuals and stock brokers for the purchase of shares in publicly quoted companies. Also most banks were engaged in buying their own shares with depositors' funds when the stock market crashed. It was even reported that a bank on one occasion gave its subsidiary a loan of 30 billion Naira to buy its own shares to artificially boost its price in the stock market.

Next was the crash in the prices of crude oil. The oil transactions promised maximized profit instantly. Consequently, valuable funds were diverted from the real sector to make a quick profit. For bank customers who invested in petroleum importation, millions of tons of petroleum products at prices in excess of 140 USD per barrel were stored in the numerous tank farms all over Lagos when current prices had crashed to below 50 USD per barrel. For some of the customers, the funds has been diverted to non-income yielding assets, leaving the bank weakly exposed. The banks lost billions of Naira in these transactions.

Finally, there was the ever-present corporate governance, which was further weakened by the new CEOs, resulting in weaker and ineffective board oversight functions, weak internal controls, noncompliance with laid-down procedures and processes, and insider abuses, especially in credit approvals and disbursements.

From the above, it was clear that the external intervention was overdue and only drastic measures could save the banking industry from total and imminent collapse. Principles, such as integrity and fair play, had been trampled upon in a reckless disregard, and things hitherto con-sidered sacred were treated with scorn. In their greed and lust for power, the bankers, just like the sycophant politicians, in this Machiavellian orchestra forgot that whatever a man sows, he shall reap. So they fell from grace to grass.

Another part of the private sector adversely affected in the decade was the stock market. For some years, the stock market in Nigeria had consistently grown and rewarded investors in an equitable manner until around 2006 when the indices started showing some signs of manipulations. It started with the massive going public of companies hitherto unknown in the sector. The procedure was very simple: the management of the companies, in what seems to be an active connivance with the regulatory authority, were allowed to sell their shares publicly without adequate preparation and due process. Once the sale was concluded and before the share certificates were released, the price of the stock was manipulated in such a manner that it would gain maximum points on each trading day.

How did this happen? Through sheer manipulation of the laws of demand and supply. Because these companies were relatively new in the stock market, their shares were held by a relatively small number of people who controlled the supply. With increasing demand by our gullible investors and through manipulations, the price of the stock would rise continuously. I use the word gullible because most investors did nothing to improve their knowledge of the stock market but were victims of a bandwagon effect. Thus there was no correlation between the companies' performances and the share price fluctuations.

As if the above fraud was not enough, insider trading was going on unpunished. I can't recall where and when the regulatory authorities sanctioned any major player in the subsector for insider abuse. Consequently, as earlier stated above, banks and other companies actively engaged in buying up their own shares to improve the prices of their shares on the floor of the stock market. It was, therefore, not surprising that when the stock market crashed in the face of the global meltdown, it dragged with it the major active banks who were culprits of this monumental corporate abuse and fraud.

The final blow on the private sector was the impact of the uncoordinated shoddy effect of the privatization exercise of the federal government of Nigeria during the decade in question. While there are some positive sides to the privatization policy, most notably in the Telecoms subsector, there was no place that a flagrant abuse of office was exhibited more than in this sector. The story of Transcorp (the new owner of Nicon Hilton Hotel, and the sale of NITEL among other public assets by government fiat) is still fresh in our memories. Billions of Naira were made on the floor of the Nigerian Stock Exchange by the initial investors, or do I say converters of our public assets (Transcorp), when they sold their hyped-up shares through the process explained above.

How does one explain a situation where very highly placed public office holders, including the President of the country, the Director General of the Nigerian Stock Exchange, and other highly placed individuals, convert public assets to themselves in the name of privatization? That was substantially what happened with Transcorp PLC.

Yet, even when those facts became public, nothing happened. Nobody has so far been prosecuted. Looking at the above scenarios, it is very clear that the public sector rot, abuse, impunity, fraud, and other crimes without pun-ishment was effectively transferred to the private sector during the decade in question.

THE SICK PRESIDENT

—◦✲◦—

There is nothing wrong with the President of the Federal Republic of Nigeria being sick. After all, he is human. But what was wrong is the way sycophants in government turned this unfortunate incident to their own benefit to the detriment of the entire nation.

Very simply, if the ministers pronounce the President incapacitated, the constitutional provision would apply, and the Vice President would become the President with its adverse consequences on ministerial appointments. In other words, some, possibly most of the ministers, would certainly lose their appointments in the new cabinet to be formed.

No wonder, the attorney general could boldly tell Nigerians that the President could rule the country from any part of the world. What a self-serving opinion by the number-one law officer of the country.

LET ME START BY RESTATING THE FACT that there is nothing wrong with the President of the Federal Republic of Nigeria being sick. After all, he is human and susceptible to all human afflictions. But what was wrong was the way sycophants in government turned this unfortunate incident to their own benefits to the detriment of the entire nation. From the inception of his administration, Nigerians had known that their President was sick. Recall the infamous public telephone call by the Emperor during a political campaign rally to the President, then a PDP presidential candidate; where the Emperor had asked the President to confirm to Nigerians on the phone that he (Umoru) was not dead from his far-away hospital bed in Germany.

Without notice and a proper hand-over to his Vice President, the President had left the country in November of 2009, just like on his previous medical trips abroad. The only difference this time was that the President was out of the country for more than ninety days. At a point, it was rumored in the papers that the President was clinically dead. This prompted a hurriedly scheduled interview with the BBC where the President spoke directly to a BBC reporter on the phone to dispel the death rumor.

The Constitution of the Federal Republic of Nigeria stipulates incapacitation as one of the grounds for removing a president. A review of what was going on would reveal that the sycophants had misconstrued the word incapacitation to mean death. Therefore, as long as the President was still breathing, he would continue to be president whether or not he was in the right state of mind to perform his presidential duties as stipulated in the constitution. What do you expect in a situation where the power to decide whether the President is incapacitated or not lies solely with his self-serving cabinet members?

In a country like Nigeria, where most ministers are corrupt, incompetent, and act with impunity even in the active presence of their supervisor—the President of the Federal Republic of Nigeria and Commander-in-Chief of the armed forces, you can imagine what would be happening when there is no supervisor. This is more like asking a man to fire himself from his plum job where there are no easier alternatives to bring food on the table.

Very simple, if the ministers pronounce the President incapacitated, the constitutional provision would apply, and the Vice President would become the President with its adverse consequences on their ministerial appointments. In other words, some or most of the ministers would certainly lose their appointments in the new cabinet to be formed.

No wonder, the attorney general could boldly tell Nigerians that the President could rule the country from any part of the world, irrespective of the state of his health, how long he had been absent from the country, or his ability or capacity to carry out his constitutional functions. What a self-serving opinion by the number-one law officer of the country?.

RECOMMENDED
WAY FORWARD

———✿✿✿———

HAVING REVIEWED THE EVENTS OF THE decade ending in 2009, I have come to the one inescapable conclusion that we, as Nigerians, can no longer continue in our present path if we are to survive as a nation and grow our economy to face the challenges of the future. We must, therefore, confront head-on the maladies weighing us down, thereby making sustainable development a reality in our nation.

Top on this list is the issue of the *restructure* of the federal constitution to guarantee the federating units' equality of all people of the nation, with more powers devolved to the units to take control of their destiny and controlling and developing their resources, while still maintaining a central government with specific functions. A truly national conference to address this very important issue would be the desired way to go to achieve true federalism.

Second on the list is *leadership*. Remember the phrase God made in response to the complaints by some African leaders against Nigeria: "Wait until you see the people that I will put in there." What seemed like a joke at the beginning of this book has been shown to be a reality. There is no doubt in any Nigerian's mind now that something is terribly wrong with our rulers and most of the ruled.

No meaningful development will occur until we take our destiny in our own hands to elect a leader who will move the nation forward. Below are some of the simple attributes of my envisioned leader:

It is one who is a patriotic, selfless, and greedless, tough-skinned, and strong-willed but a compassionate leader who understands the sufferings of Nigerians and is willing and determined to change the course of history and minimize emphasis on his or her bank account.

The person must be guided by the principle of equity and fairness, especially to the downtrodden masses and to the various sections of the country that have suffered and are still suffering untold hardship, neglect, and deprivation. His team must understand that "the work must be done or face the music."

He or she must be committed to the principle of separation of powers as would be enshrined in our constitution and be willing to take immediate action to implement true federalism.

The leader must understand the difference between patriotism, loyalty, and sycophancy and would encourage and reward the former while frowning and sanctioning the latter.

The leader would be ready to make the supreme sacrifice, including laying down his life in his quest for the betterment of all Nigerians.

This leader need not be a genius as problems facing the nation are still at the primary stages of provision of electric power, water, roads, housing, food, and health care. But he must have basic understanding of how national economies operate.

On the other hand, the *followers* must begin to resist sycophantic traits among themselves. They must educate themselves to know the adverse effects of their praise-singing and hero-worshipping attitude toward their corrupt leaders to their communities and the nation in general.

The followers must begin to collectively express strong dislike for leaders who have taken undue advantage of them. They must even show greater disgust at the leaders' flaunting their ill-gotten committed by our leaders would have been greatly minimized if they knew that the public would be entitled to all the information in their (leaders) decision-making processes. The public must therefore put pressure on all agents of the government to implement the Freedom of the Press Bill (FOPB).

I believe that if we conscientiously and collectively apply these simple recommendations in a fair, equitable, and consistent manner, we will begin to reposition our great nation on the path of sustainable development.

www.ingramcontent.com/pod-product-compliance
Lightning Source LLC
Chambersburg PA
CBHW022105020426
42335CB00012B/834